SHAPING YOUR WORKPLACE CULTURE

A practical guide

Vanessa O'Shea

Culture Shapers Publications

Published by Culture Shapers Publications

ISBN: 978-1-790-20622-3

Copyright © 2018 Vanessa O'Shea

A CIP record for this book is available from the British Library

The moral right of the author has been asserted

Edited and typeset by Helen Jones
Graphic design by Jules Burt (We Will Run)

CONTENTS

Acknowledgements

I want to thank the friends who have supported and encouraged me and those who have read my draft and given me feedback. I want to thank my children and those in your generation. You have been the inspiration for me to use my time to try to improve your future working environment.

Thanks to my husband Ric, who believed in me and encouraged me to keep going all the way through the writing process.

Special thanks to my friend John; without our monthly check-ins, I probably wouldn't have written this book.

Preface

I have a vision of the future. I see people who are using their strengths and talents to make a difference in the world. They belong to a group of people who are doing the same; and in doing so they are finding meaning in their lives.

They look forward to being at work because their workplace is a place where this happens.

I also see organisations that are producing excellent products and services. They are innovative, forward-thinking and competitive. They operate in a long-sighted way ensuring they don't damage the environment. They are generous with their staff, and positively impact local communities and society at large.

People are queuing up to work for them.

Then, there is the bit in the middle, the area that connects these two parts. It's the space that generates the conditions for those individuals to grow. In doing so, it captures and channels passion, creativity, energy and enthusiasm. People are fulfilled. They don't have to wait until their retirement until they do what they really want to do.

The bit in the middle is called workplace culture and it is what this book is about.

INTRODUCTION

There is an expression that we often use if we are responsible for people or organisations. It's a value statement that would suggest high priority in how our organisations or teams are run; a phrase that implies that people come first. It's a declaration we may strongly subscribe to but not necessarily know how to follow through on. It is:

Our people are our best assets

When this statement is carried out in practice, our workplaces look like this:

- People's natural talents, passions and motivations are known, and projects are delegated accordingly.

- Time, and sometimes money, is spent on developing individuals e.g. coaching, mentoring, and delegation of significant tasks.

- There are a high proportion of internal promotions.

- Mission and expectations are clear, so individuals know how to contribute meaningfully.

- Remuneration and benefits are equitable across the organisation.

- Staff well-being is catered for, in, for example, flexible working, wellness days, health checks, creativity workshops.

- People are queuing up to work for us.

When this statement isn't carried out in practice, however, our workplaces look more like this:

- We don't know what our people's natural talents, passions or dreams are.

- There is regular underperformance and lack of loyalty.

- There's a disproportionate pay gap, or benefits, between top line management and front-line staff.

- One-to-one reviews, supervision, or regular time dedicated to meeting with individuals isn't prioritised.

- Ideas and suggestions from all levels aren't invited.

- There are instances of stress-related absence.

- We struggle to recruit and hold on to talented people.

Our people are our best assets. How do we follow through on that statement? If your experience is more aligned to the second list, then there is some work to do. Just as a seed needs certain conditions to grow well, we as human beings also need certain conditions to flourish. The good news is that we can facilitate that growth by creating an environment or *culture* that nurtures people, so they feel valued, they bring more of themselves to work, and they are released into contributing towards fulfilling the organisation's mission.

From small charities to large corporate organisations, workplace culture is being highlighted as of key significance in how they fulfil their purpose.

This book presents a four-step culture-shaping model that you can read in a couple of ways:

- *As a reference book* – delving into it, implementing different elements as and when you need it.

- *In its entirety* – working through it step-by-step, if you want to follow a complete process.

How you use this book will depend on how much help you need, how much time there is available, your people resource, the support for the process, and what level of influence you have in your organisation.

When to read this book:

There isn't a bad time to invest in improving your organisation's culture; but there are specific times when culture shaping is particularly useful. This would include:

- Starting out; setting the culture you would want to have early on.

- Anticipating growth, opening another site; ensuring that your culture is continued across new locations.

- Preparing for a merger; bringing two cultures together, finding the common values.

- Taking a periodic review of your purpose, progress.

- Simply wanting to be a better employer.

This book is for you if:

You are responsible for developing the organisation or people. You may be the Head of People or Training & Development, a Consultant brought in to advise or facilitate change, a Team Leader or a CEO. Whilst it is the most senior positions that have the most influence – and responsibility – to create a positive culture, this book is also for you if you simply want to work in a healthy, happy, thriving culture. This culture-shaping model was developed in a company with around fifty people. However, if you work in a larger organisation, it's possible to shape a culture within your team; therefore this book is also for you.

This book is not for you if:

You are aligning a culture-shaping exercise to quick financial targets. We all want to get the most out of the resources we have. Culture, however, has a life of its own and will evolve. Incidentally, there is increasing evidence that it will improve the organisation's finances.(See Chapter 1, 4 Organisational success'.)

How this book differs from other books about business culture:

There are four key differences about this book from other books about culture:

Firstly, it's concise. At around twenty thousand words, it is under half the size of most business books.

Secondly, it's written from the perspective of someone who has worked in an HR office. (Prior to being a consultant, I worked in HR for 20 years.) In an HR department (that is welcoming and supportive) you often hear what people *really* think about leadership, decisions made, and the personal impact on individuals. Sometimes, you see a 'less than healthy culture' being a contributory factor in a resignation, or, alarmingly, in a capability issue.

Thirdly, whilst this book can be scaled up to a large organisation, the experience that I have leant on is one of working in small and medium-size organisations. Most other books about culture are written with large corporate organisations in mind which can be hard to relate or adapt to, if you work for a smaller organisation.

Finally, and most importantly, this book is a practical model. There are plenty of inspiring books available about culture that present success stories. Whilst they may give tips and ideas, they don't often present a model that you can apply to the workplace.

Structure

Part 1 (chapters 1–2) of the book will present some real examples of positive and negative cultures; the rewards and benefits to individuals and to the wider organisation. It will also list some factors for success. In this section, I will also be introducing you to my model for shaping a positive culture.

Part 2 (chapters 3–8) of the book will walk you through each of the four stages of culture shaping.

This book is written as a practical guide, one that you can use to create a positive culture. Therefore, there is a checklist for action at the end of each chapter. You will also find a summary at the end of each chapter, summarising the key messages to help you pull all the information together.

As people, we come with a unique package of life experiences, perceptions, skills, talents, passions and dreams. Most of us spend the majority of our waking hours at work. As leaders and managers, I believe we have a responsibility to make that time worthwhile, for everyone.

My aim in writing this book and presenting this culture-shaping model is to enable us to action the belief that people are our best resources so that our people will be more fulfilled, motivated and engaged. Our organisations will reap the benefits.

Summary

- ☐ Declaring 'our people are our best assets' doesn't necessarily mean that they are. Shaping a culture in which people are valued, and therefore thrive, can make this a reality.

- ☐ This book is designed for you to work through as a step-by-step process, or to use as a reference book and dip in to chapters as and when you need to.

- ☐ This book is for you if you want to work in a culture in which you, and those you have responsibility for, can flourish.

- ☐ This book is possibly not for you if you just want to achieve quick results and targets.

- ☐ This book is different from other books about business culture because it is concise, written from the perspective of an HR professional, more easily applied to small and medium-sized companies and it is a practical model, with detailed processes.

PART ONE:
THE BACKGROUND

Chapter 1

Workplace Culture: What it Means and Why it Matters

The First Day at Work

It's Alice's first day in her new job in Future Kids. Her manager has taken her around the building and introduced her to her colleagues. She has been shown her workspace, the location of the kitchen/fire exit/W.C. and has now been left reading the Policies folder. Alice goes to make a cup of coffee and gets chatting to someone.

She asks them 'What's it like working here?' They tell her not to engage Barbara in finance in a political debate – she is dismissive of views other than her own, and it will get heated; people tend to hide their mistakes; ideas aren't invited, so if you have one, email it directly to the CEO; working hours are 9–5pm, but if you want to progress make sure you aren't seen leaving before 5.20pm; and stay away from Bob at work socials, as he will give inappropriate hugs. (He's senior so no one really talks about it.)

Alice is glad she asked, because she hadn't read this information in the staff handbook. She then notices the values on the wall. They are: courtesy, continuous learning, innovation, work–life balance and transparency. When introduced to the CEO she mentions this contradiction.

What you have just experienced is Future Kids' culture; possibly not the one they would aspire to, but it's the one they have.

Culture 101

Culture describes the environment in which behaviours are either encouraged, or not tolerated. It's the result of a group's values, beliefs, traditions, taboos, and written and unwritten rules. From different nationalities and religions, to families, sports teams, friendship circles, and workplaces, culture exists wherever people come together to form a group to which there is a purpose and a sense of belonging.

Whilst rules that are written down (if known and followed) can influence a culture, e.g. policies and procedures, it most often manifests in those unspoken rules of behaviour. What we want to be versus what we actually are.

Problems can arise when there's a gap between what you are told to be true, i.e. we value and consider every new idea, we treat everyone with courtesy and respect, we address any taboo issues, and our people are our best assets; and what you experience to be true.

Because it's what you experience, rather than what you are told, that you believe to be true.

In those scenarios, we are in danger of losing talented people, because we create a culture where people feel unvalued and unappreciated. In *Daring Greatly*[1], Brene Brown describes this as 'the disengagement divide… when (those that lead us) aren't living up to their end of the social contract'.

Culture DNA

Finding the culture that is right for you is crucial. There is no harm in bringing in a pool table, keeping the fridge stocked up with food, or offering a subsidised gym membership. However, the way that other organisations demonstrate their culture, isn't necessarily right for you. Introducing 'beer o' clock' on Fridays may fit with a media company's value of fun but may not work for an accountancy firm. In addition, it may not deal with some of the deeper reasons why you don't have a positive culture. These perks may be well received but having them doesn't mean that you have resolved the culture issue.

In my view, the two main approaches to creating a positive culture (and those addressed in this book) are:

1. for an organisation to put its values into action

   and

2. to develop in its leaders the qualities needed to shape a positive culture.

Why does workplace culture matter?

1 People are valuable

The type of people issues that occur in most workplaces and those which are likely to keep the HR department busy include formal processes to do with low performance, absence, disciplinary and grievance. In addition to these, there are the subtler issues, such as doing the minimum (presenteeism), attitude problems, regular one or two days' absence, or just general low morale. These are just as problematic, but much harder to address.

This withdrawal of oneself often masks dissatisfaction and can be a symptom of a deeper unease. Sometimes this happens when the organisation's strategy takes priority over its people. For example, at a time of growth, when the priority is acquiring new sites, takeovers etc., the danger is that people are then required to fit into the jobs needed to get there. Whilst there may be an argument for this in the short term, it can cause us to treat people as commodities, rather than unique individuals with valuable contributions to make.

If you don't feel valued, or appreciated, then you're not going to give any more than you have to. To put it bluntly, you aren't going to care, because your employer isn't demonstrating care for you. Happily, the reverse is true. If you feel valued, and appreciated this is usually reciprocated in effort, time and loyalty.

2 People are unique and have an individual purpose

> *'Talent of all kinds is lurking in our organisations; we need to create a climate of freedom to unleash it.'*
> *Bob Chapman/Raj Sisodia;* Everybody Matters[2]

As individuals, we are one-offs, with diverse strengths, passions, skills, qualities, personalities and backgrounds; and, a purpose in this life. Is it possible to align this wealth of individual resource and purpose to the organisation's mission? You would need to know what your people's strengths are in order to do that.

Strengths

Tom Rath's book, *StrengthsFinder 2.0*[3], based on Gallup's extensive research on strengths, suggests that when people aren't working to their strengths, they 'dread going to work, treat their customers poorly, are less creative, and tell everyone what a miserable company they work for'.

However, when we do something we enjoy, motivation soars, time flies and work flows. Work becomes easier, and we perform better, because we are tapping into our natural talents.

Mark Twain once described a man who dies and meets Saint Peter at the Pearly Gates. Knowing that Saint Peter was very wise, he asked a question that he had wondered about all his life. He said, 'Saint Peter, I have been interested in military history for many years. Who was the greatest general of all time?' Saint Peter quickly responded, 'Oh, that's a simple question; it's that man right over there.' 'You must be mistaken,' responded the man, now very perplexed. 'I knew that man on earth; he was just a common labourer.' 'That's right, my friend,' Saint Peter assured him. 'He would have been the greatest general of all time, *if he had been a general.*'[4]

Sometimes you meet people who are fulfilling their purpose in life; but the way that most of us can't wait for work to finish, so we can do what we *really* want to do, would suggest that most people aren't.

The right culture can create an environment where those untapped talents and strengths can be released, bringing fulfilment to individuals and success to the organisation.

3 A good workplace culture benefits the wider society

When we are fulfilled at work our health, family, community and society benefits. Knowing that we are doing something that taps into our natural talents and skills brings enjoyment and fulfilment. We are making a difference to the world, no matter how small, through our work contribution. We have a sense of *meaning*. We are happier and healthier. The medical profession recognises that our mental state affects us physiologically; the extent of stress-related absence provides evidence to this.

If we treat people well, they will feel better about themselves and in turn treat the others in their lives well. In his book *Everybody Matters*, Bob Chapman describes the moment when he saw how impactful their culture work at Barry-Wehmiller had been. When asked what difference the workplace culture had made to his life, an employee on his manufacturing line said, 'my wife talks to me'. He went on to say:

'People ask me what I think; they listen to me and I actually have a chance to impact things, including my own job. When I feel respected, I feel pretty good about myself; I'm nicer to my wife. And when I'm nicer to my wife she talks to me.'

4 Organisational success

The impact of having a positive culture at work doesn't just have personal and societal benefits.

Pursuit Marketing, based in Glasgow, addressed their work–life balance by reducing their days to four per week, but continuing to pay the staff full time. Lorraine Gray, Operations Director, says, 'The culture in the workplace drives better results, better performance, and a happier workforce. So, our retention rates are really high. We can attract the best talent. When our staff are in the office, they're far more productive. They're focussed on what they need to do.' [5]

And what about this for an outcome? Since they reduced their days, their turnover has increased from £2.2m in 2016 to £5m, as of the beginning of 2018. Taking brave steps to address the organisation's work–life balance has tapped into their people's motivation, resulting in greater productivity, bringing financial gain.

Some common cultures

What follows is an outline of some of the most common cultures that appear in our workplaces; you may be able to think of some others. See if you can spot any signs of them in *your* workplace.

Culture	Focus	Outcome	Impact on organisation
Positivity	What are the ideas and solutions?	Enthusiasm, energetic team dynamics	Attract talented people, increased organisation strength
Versus			
Negativity	What can I criticise?	Gossip, moaning, lack of personal responsibility	Lack of growth, division (us and them)

Culture	Focus	Outcome	Impact on organisation
Learning (through mistakes)	What part did I play?	Individual development, energy, motivation	Innovation, growth
Versus			
Blame	Who can we scapegoat?	Fear of taking risks, cover up of mistakes	Division (us and them), lack of growth

Culture	Focus	Outcome	Impact on organisation
Strength	How can I empower others to their potential?	Growth, motivation, enjoyment	Greater productivity, team cohesion
Versus			
Weakness	How can we create perfect people?	Low morale, lack of transparency	Lack of growth, 'stress' absence

Culture	Focus	Outcome	Impact on organisation
Trust	How can people use their own judgements?	Optimism, cooperation, team synergy	Good reputation 'can-do'
Versus			
Cynicism	How can we control people?	High level of rules, bureaucracy	Lack of growth and innovation

Culture	Focus	Outcome	Impact on organisation
Integrity	What is the right thing to do?	Respect, loyalty, goodwill	Growth, talented people stay
Versus			
Disconnect	What is the right thing to say?	Hypocritical, distrust of management	Poor reputation, good people leave

How do you enable your people to develop in their unique strengths and talents? Create an environment or culture in which your people can grow.

Seven factors for success

Here are seven key factors for successfully implementing a culture-shaping programme:

- Modelling: the CEO and senior staff are committed to, and live out the new culture, because if you want a positive culture leaders need to embody it.

- Investment: there is commitment to investing time and financial resources in training managers to become better managers.

- Allies: you are able to identify people who understand and support the culture-shaping process and can therefore cascade the programme through the organisation. This is crucial to your culture spreading to all parts of the organisation.

- Values: you know what your values are and believe in them. If you aren't clear on your values, there are some exercises in Chapter 4 to identify them.

- Patience: you don't shortcut the model and jump to behaviour control. You need to allow your teams to identify their own behavioural norms.

- Persistence: it's a process that takes time. You may have to undo some set cultures, so be prepared to keep going.

- Bravery: when you are encouraging people to take risks and stretch themselves it takes courage to allow them to occasionally fail.

I will expand on these as we go through the book, but I want to emphasise them at this early stage.

Finally, if you are feeling overwhelmed by the task ahead, take heart; just one person's efforts can begin to shape a culture. In a highly bureaucratic and controlled organisation, a friend gets a job as Head of Marketing. Met with a 'closed-door' culture, he starts to leave his door ajar, and every day he draws a small picture on his whiteboard. Passers-by become intrigued and start to enter his office, saying 'what's with the picture?'

A bit of fun and creativity brought human interaction back and began to influence the culture.

Conclusion

Our culture is essentially the environment in which certain behaviours are deemed acceptable and not acceptable. Culture is *experienced* and reflects our actual values, not those we aspire to, or state. It is unique, as it is reflected slightly differently by each individual within it. It can be shaped to one that is right for your organisation.

This chapter has been about raising awareness of how culture reveals itself in the workplace. This first set of actions consists of questions for reflection, to enable you to gain a picture of your current culture and begin to imagine what you would like it to be.

Summary

- ☐ Culture determines behaviour and is the result of a group's values, beliefs, traditions, taboos, and written and unwritten rules.

- ☐ When there's a gap between what you experience and what you are told to be true, people can withdraw and become distrustful and disengaged.

- ☐ As you show value to people, they will more likely work to their strengths. They will feel fulfilled, and the organisation and society will benefit.

- ☐ Some common cultures include:
  - Positivity/negativity
  - Learning/blame
  - Strength/weakness
  - Trust/cynicism
  - Integrity/disconnect

- ☐ Successful culture shaping involves:
  - Leadership modelling the right culture
  - Investment in time and finance
  - Generating allies amongst the workforce
  - Knowing your values
  - Patience
  - Persistence
  - Bravery

Action Checklist 1

Culture 101

Ask yourself the following questions:

What is it like to work here? Answer in terms of: people to avoid/ work–life balance/elephants in the room/level of autonomy etc.

....

....

....

What are your stated values?

....

....

What are your actual values?

....

....

Culture DNA

What are your organisational perks?

....

Do they motivate people to do their best work?

....

If so how?

....

Why does workplace culture matter?

Do you know what *your* strengths are? If so, list them below:

....

....

....

Do you know what *your team* strengths are? If so, list some of them below:

....

....

....

Common cultures

Which of the cultures outlined have you/are you experiencing?

....

....

What aspects of positive culture would you like to see in your workplace?

....

....

Finally, positive culture starts with you. Name one action you are going to take that aligns with this positive culture:

....

....

CHAPTER 2

The Culture-Shaping Model: An Overview

The Culture-Shaping Model[6]

We all want our people to perform well. However, if we try to control behaviour by prescribing it down to the detail, people will feel stifled and restrained. This culture-shaping model seeks to do the opposite. It is designed to create the environment in which people have the *freedom* to demonstrate the organisation's purpose and values in their job. The detail will depend on their individual personalities, strengths and talents.

If we look at it this way, culture has a personality of its own.

Stage 1: What – Mission

Your mission is *what* you do. Included in mission is your purpose and vision.

Purpose

Your purpose comes from seeing a gap, or a problem, and wanting to create a solution. It's what motivates you to get out of bed in the morning. You believe that something different or new needs to happen, and you have to believe in it. It's the answer to the question 'why does this organisation exist?'

It anchors you when you go about planning and making decisions regarding your mission. Clarifying and regularly communicating it is important as it's a big motivator for you and your people.

Vision

Closely linked to purpose is the vision. Your vision is how you imagine the world being a better place in 5, 10, 20 years' time as a result of that product, service, improvement or solution.

The next step in shaping your culture is to clarify and communicate your mission. Your people need to understand the organisation's mission and consequently how their role contributes to it. Once they know why their role exists, then you will be tapping into a rich source of intrinsic motivation.

Your mission determines how you are going to deploy your skills, talents, energy and time to bring about your vision. On a practical level, it's important to clearly articulate your mission for the following reasons:

- You know if your organisation is succeeding in what it was created to do.

- You can be accountable or responsible for seeing it happen.

As you translate your mission to teams and roles, your people are clear as to their roles and how they progress the mission.

Stage 2: Why – Values

The next step is to identify your values. Your values explain *why* you do what you do, in the way that you do it. These are your principles, those things you hold in (the most) high regard in all that you do, whether in your personal life or at work. Values make up your organisational DNA; they give you your identity. They should be reflected in every action taken.

Why does a business need a set of values? They provide a sense of common purpose and ensure that there is a consistency in how people carry out their roles and responsibilities. They give you and your people guidance as to how to fulfil roles, which in turn will fulfil your mission. Just as your personal values are revealed in how you live your life, your organisational values will be revealed in how people, for example, communicate, relate to each other, make decisions etc.

As we saw in chapter one, your stated values may not be your intended values. It is therefore in your best interest to decide, clarify and communicate your values.

Stage 3: How – Embedding our Values

Embedding values means taking those principles described in 'Stage 2' and putting them into action, from the top down. This stage is about *how* you put your values into action. This is the process of embedding values into the fabric of the organisation. It involves exploring, with your people, how they have an impact on attitude, approach and behaviour, thereby creating 'norms' that will form your culture.

Unless you are intentional about embedding your values, it's likely that they will remain on your website, in your staff handbook or in your head, and have little impact on the organisation. Investing time and resources in this stage will contribute significantly towards shaping a culture that is strong and long-lasting.

Stage 4: Who – Equipping Managers

The fourth stage of the culture-shaping model consists of a development programme designed to train managers in the character traits they need to develop so they play their part in creating a thriving culture. It's *who* has most influence in the development of a healthy culture. Leadership supersedes job titles; anyone, in any role can display leadership qualities. With that in mind, the programme can eventually be rolled out to all staff. However, it's the behaviour of those in positions of management that will have the most influence on the culture.

Culture

If you have followed the previous stages, at this point you can observe the resulting culture, which will look something like this:

■ Your people will be intrinsically motivated to do their best because they believe in the organisation's purpose.

■ As you have communicated your mission, and what role they play in fulfilling it, they will know how to contribute to the success of the organisation. As they do this, they will feel good about themselves, fulfilled.

■ Your people will carry out their roles in a way that reflects your values, not because you have told them how to behave, but because they will have explored how what they do demonstrates the organisation's values.

Conclusion

Shaping culture doesn't end once you have grown a positive culture. It is constantly evolving, as organisations evolve, and people come and go. Therefore, the model is a continuous one and should be periodically revisited.

The following chapters will walk you through each element of the cycle, starting with 'mission'.

Summary

- [ ] This four-stage culture model allows people the freedom to demonstrate the organisation's purpose and values; therefore, the culture that evolves is unique.

- [ ] Mission (what you do). Included in mission, is your purpose and vision. Purpose is why your organisation exists; vision describes how you see things being different and mission is what you do to realise your vision.

- [ ] Values (why you do what you do). Your values are the principles that you intend to build your business on.

- [ ] Embedding your values (how you put your values into action). This is the process of ensuring that your values inform everything you do.

- [ ] Equipping managers (who have the most influence in shaping culture). This consists of a management programme designed to help your managers develop seven qualities of a culture-shaping leader.

- [ ] The resulting culture should be one that generates an identity that reflects the organisation's purpose and values.

PART TWO:
THE MECHANICS

CHAPTER 3
What: Mission

Back at Future Kids, the Communications Officer Andy, who has been in post since the charity was founded, is putting together the Annual Report and has located its mission statement. It says:

To provide a service that enables local 12- to 18-year-olds to transition into emotionally, physically and socially healthy adults in collaboration with the local community.

He was surprised to notice that it was still pretty relevant ten years on.

Mission

 What you do (and why) + how you do it = your culture.

In the cycle of culture shaping, articulating your mission comes first. What you do (your mission) and why you do it (your purpose) are two questions which require different answers. Organisations, however, usually merge the two answers into the term *mission*.

'A small team, committed to a cause bigger than themselves, can achieve absolutely anything.' Simon Sinek

Simon Sinek's book *Start with Why*[7] comprehensively describes the importance of knowing your purpose – your 'why'. Knowing why you do what you do will help you to articulate what action you are going to take – your mission. Articulating your purpose will also inform your people as to why their roles exist and therefore how they can contribute to the fulfilling of the company's purpose.

Once you know your why, you can define what actions you will take to fulfil it.

Some questions to ask yourself when defining your purpose are:

■ What product have you bought that you were dissatisfied with?

■ What service have you encountered that was less than satisfactory?

■ What is the problem you want to solve?

Or simply,

- What idea do you have that will make the world a better place?

Costa Coffee's[8] purpose is to save the world from mediocre coffee. Their mission is to be the most successful coffee business anywhere in the world as measured by customer preference and return on investment.

John Lewis'[9] ultimate purpose is the happiness of all its members, through their worthwhile and satisfying employment in a successful business. It does this by running a business in which the responsibilities of ownership, as well as its rewards – profit, knowledge and power – are shared.

Walt Disney's[10] purpose was to bring a smile to a child's face. The mission of the Walt Disney Company is to be one of the world's leading producers and providers of entertainment and information.

A third element to mention here is the *vision*. Being able to *visualise* the world being different because of your product/service/idea is crucial. And, of course, vision just stays in your imagination unless you act on it.

- Martin Luther King[11] imagined a world where all mankind could live in peace; he led a civil rights movement that led to the 1964 Civil Rights Act.

- William Wilberforce[12] imagined a world without slavery; he worked for 20 years until he pushed through legislation abolishing slavery.

- Millicent Fawcett[13] imagined a world where women had equal rights; she spent her life campaigning for women to be able to vote.

These three were fuelled by the injustice they witnessed and experienced.

Here are a couple of visionary leaders in the world of business, and the arts:

- John Spedan Lewis[14] had a vision to create a better form of business and actioned this by signing away his personal ownership rights to his employees (partners).

- JK Rowling[15], as a single parent living on welfare benefits in Glasgow, Scotland, had a vision that she would be a writer; so she wrote.

Being visionary gives you licence to dream the impossible. People aren't motivated by the knowledge that they are making their employer more financially profitable; they need to know that there is a higher purpose to which they are contributing.

Future Kids

Nicola had founded Future Kids years ago. As a youth leader herself, she had been particularly taken by the idea of 'it takes a village to raise a child'. She had therefore designed the service around significant connections between members of the local community and its young people. It had grown over the years, and now employed forty staff with a youth membership of over five hundred young people. Its activities included the following:

- It ran clubs such as art, science, drama, running and football, all facilitated by local people.

- The drama and dance clubs would go into local retirement homes and perform pieces they had learnt.

- Students from the local music college gave free music lessons.

- The local college of technology ran a gaming club and lessons on coding.

- Local coffee shops offered the older children barista training and, once they were old enough, part-time work.

- Local charities offered opportunities for young people to serve on their board of trustees.

- Retired business consultants delivered workshops on how to write a CV and complete an application form.

- The local chamber of commerce offered five hours per week coaching sessions on how to build confidence.

- A nurse from the local GP surgery ran information sessions on health and well-being.

With all this fantastic work, as often happens, there had been little focus on shaping an internal workplace culture that fully reflected the charity's values.

Conclusion

Mission statements are the result of your vision, your purpose and the action you are going to take. They should be simple, and jargon free, and give you a benchmark on which to measure your success.

Summary

☐ Your mission describes what you do, e.g. 'to provide a service that enables young people to transition into adults in collaboration with the community'.

☐ Your purpose describes why you do what you do, e.g. 'bringing a smile to a child's face'.

☐ Your vision describes how the future will be different as a result of your organisation, e.g. 'there will be a better form of business'.

☐ It is your mission that will make this vision a reality.

☐ When a charity or organisation is busy outworking its mission, a common and understandable outcome is that a culture evolves that doesn't truly reflect the organisational identity.

Action Checklist 2

Revisit or write your mission statement:

Firstly identify your *vision*: how is the world going to be different as a result of your product/service/idea?

....

....

Secondly what is your *purpose*: why do we do what we do?

....

....

What is your *mission*: how do we outwork our purpose?

....

....

....

CHAPTER 4
Why: Values

Back at Future Kids, following the conversation with Alice, Nicola the CEO is somewhat alarmed and has decided to do some work around shaping culture. She starts by reflecting on the values of the charity and why they are important.

Future Kids works in a community that is diverse in age, faith and nationality, with a range of social and economic differences. Communicating respect for others' opinions, beliefs and perceptions was essential for their work to take place. *Courtesy* was the first value.

Nicola understood that for innovation and excellence to occur people needed the freedom to grow in their knowledge, understanding and skills; mistakes were part of growth. *Continuous Learning* was the second value.

Future Kids' vision would not be realised unless they were able to tap into the wealth of experience, skills and wisdom of the local community. *Collaboration* was the third value.

As a working parent she understood how being able to work flexibly, whether it be for parental or caring responsibilities or being able to enjoy life by not working full-time, resulted in happier people who in return brought their best to the workplace. *Work–life balance* was the fourth value.

She found that being upfront about her weaknesses, rather than losing the respect of her staff, won it. She also realised that developing honest channels of communication soon exposed those 'elephants in the room'. *Transparency* was the fifth value.

Values

As we saw in chapter 2, your values are those things you hold in (the most) high regard in all that you do, both in your personal and work life.

Let's take our *personal* values.

Values derive from our personal experience, our belief system or life philosophy and are usually very deep-rooted.

A good way to identify what our personal values are is to ask ourselves the question: what behaviour can't I tolerate in other people?

It may be that you hate it when someone pulls out in front of you when you are driving and then slows down: *consideration for others*. It may bother you greatly when people constantly moan about their jobs but don't make any effort to go and find another one: *courage*. How about when a talented young employee (previously overlooked by their manager) is poached by a competitor who spots their potential: *empowerment*. Or when someone is stuck in their ways and unwilling to update their skill set to keep up with current developments: *growth*. Or when a manager makes a decision that goes wrong and he/she blames everyone else: *personal accountability*.

Another way to identify what we value most is how we spend our time and our money. For more insight, take a look at your diary, and your credit/bank statement.

Values steer our relationship choices, decisions and direction in life, whether we are conscious of them or not.

If for example, we value justice we may go into the legal profession, police force, or set up a charity supporting a particular cause. If we value caring for people, we may go into nursing or HR. If we value attention to detail we may become an account-ant. And if we value creativity we may pursue life as an artist, writer or garden designer.

Just as we as individuals have values, so can a group of individuals.

Organisational values

Why does an organisation need a set of values?

The main reason is so that staff can understand the principles that are underlying the organisation's purpose. Being aware of their employer's values will help them appreciate what the or-ganisation is about, why it exists.

Having a set of values is also vital to ensure that there is a con-sistency in how people carry out their roles and responsibilities. If you ask your staff to come up with their own ways in which they can action the values in their roles this will result in a self-determined standard to how each staff member approaches their work. People would adopt a certain approach not just to the tasks and responsibilities but to all areas of their working life such as their relationships with colleagues, customers, how they communicate and how they make decisions.

If individuals and teams have identified how they, for example, action 'excellence', imagine how that would affect the effective-ness of an organisation.

Values determine our behaviour. They are very effective drivers as to how we live and work. If a group shares the same values, they will develop 'norms' – acceptable and unacceptable ways of behaving. And this is what creates a culture.

A culture of disengagement

But what happens when your stated values differ from your actual values? Consider the reaction when a politician who has spoken out about integrity in politics gets caught falsifying their expenses. Or when an organisation, who state they value equality, award their senior staff another bonus that is disproportionate to everyone else.

The result is a culture that is one of distrust and disrespect because the other party hasn't lived up to their side of the social contract.

Leaders shape culture

It is extremely important that leaders fully support the organisation's values and work hard to model them in their own roles and spheres.

The reality is that culture is modelled and disproportionately influenced by the behaviour of those at the top.

If an organisation's leaders don't intentionally create a culture, then one will develop by itself over time. When a culture develops on its own there is a risk that it will be influenced and controlled by the norms, beliefs and experiences of individuals rather than the values of the organisation.

An example to learn from

This is particularly highlighted – and disturbing – when you hear about an organisation whose mission is to help those in extreme need being found to employ staff who are exploitative, abusive and bullying. This demonstrates a culture that is severely broken, with a gulf between stated values and policies, and actual practice. In cases such as these, robust, thorough safeguarding policies are essential. However, to be utilised effectively they must exist in the right culture.

If there is an organisational culture of unaccountability, indifference, bullying or aggression then even the best policies will be at best underutilised and at worst meaningless.

Leadership has the power and responsibility to promote the organisation's values, communicate policies, resource safeguarding and hold managers to account on implementation and in respect of any breaches.

Organisations don't intentionally create cultures that foster disengagement. But when there is a gap between your *actual* values and your *stated* values, this is likely to happen. Identifying your actual values may be a sobering experience, but without doing so you won't see what needs to change.

Interestingly, *Good to Great*,[16] the book that analyses the key factors that took a good company and made it great, found that the mere fact that a company has working values is enough to make it great. Jim Collins, the author says, 'It doesn't seem to matter what core values you have, but that you have core values at all; that you know what they are, that you build them explicitly into the organisation and that you preserve them over time.'

Before we get to the action page, here are some examples of organisations showing one of their values, why they have that value, and how they outwork it.

Organisation: Brightec,[17] a business that develops mobile apps

Value: Relationships

Why? Their business mission is to create a company

---

that customers love working with and employees love working for. One of their key tools for success is to create long-term relationships with their clients. This means they can grow, learn and continuously improve how they serve those clients.

They do this by: asking job applicants to complete a strengths questionnaire. Applicants that have relationship-building strengths will have a much better chance of joining the team.

Organisation: Hewlett Packard (HP)[18] a computer and electronics company

Value: Continuous improvement

Why? So they remain competitive in a fast-progressing technological world.

They do this by: issuing annual surveys containing free-form feedback; and placing targets on management for staff engagement.

Charity: Brighton Table Tennis Club[19]

Value: Community

Why? In their belief that table tennis can transform lives, they wish no part of their community to be excluded.

They do this by: putting tables in parks, squares, schools, sports centres, sheltered housing schemes, homeless centres, psychiatric hospitals and prisons.

> **Organisation:** Spotify, Digital Streaming Service[20]
>
> **Value:** Innovation
>
> **Why?** They need to be at the forefront of new technologies.
>
> **They do this by:** encouraging staff to take 10% of their time as 'hack days' to spend time trying out new ideas and staying up-to-date with new tools and techniques.

Conclusion

Your values are the necessary pillars on which to build your mission. They are your *most* important principles. Any more than five may be hard to keep track of and there may even only be one that particularly stands out. A friend, who is a head teacher in a state school, is beset by challenges such as year-on-year budget cuts and needing to accommodate more children with complex needs, requiring more resources. He realises that the only way that his teachers are able to continue working in such a challenging environment is for them to champion, encourage and support each other. Therefore, the only value he talks about is… *love*.

Summary

- ☐ Values are important aspects of fulfilling your vision and give you a unique organisational identity.

- ☐ Our personal values steer our relationship choices, decisions and direction in life.

- ☐ An organisation needs a set of values to develop a culture that is made up of 'norms': acceptable and unacceptable ways of behaving.

- ☐ A culture of disengagement occurs when stated values differ from actual values.

- ☐ If an organisation's leaders don't intentionally create and model a culture then one will develop by itself over time, which may not be the one that the organisation desires.

Action Checklist 3

Personal or Individual Values

Consider the list of values below.

Circle the words that resonate with you in your personal/professional life. Narrow them down to ten, then five. How are they demonstrated in your life? Where there is a tension in your life, can you trace it back to being out of alignment with one of your values?

List of Values

Acceptance	Family	Mindfulness
Accountability	Flexibility	Partnership
Achievement	Freedom	Passion
Adventure	Fun	Patience
Altruism	Generosity	Peace
Authenticity	Gratitude	Perseverance
Collaboration	Growth	Power
Community	Hard work	Questioning
Competition	Harmony	Reflection
Creativity	Holistic	Relationship
Curiosity	Honesty	Respect
Dependable	Honour	Responsibility
Discipline	Hope	Risk taking
Diversity	Imagination	Selflessness
Dream	Inclusivity	Solidarity
Empathy	Independence	Spontaneity

Empowerment	Individuality	Strength
Encouragement	Integrity	Tradition
Entertainment	Innovation	Transformation
Environment	Joy	Trust
Equality	Justice	Uniqueness
Excellence	Leadership	Vision
Expertise	Learning	Vulnerability
Faith	Love	Wisdom

Organisational Values

Actual Values

Your values should be authentic, relevant to the work of your organisation, and resonate with the staff team. Ask a selection of your workforce (who are willing to be truthful) the following questions taken from Brene Brown's book *Daring Greatly*[21].

What happens when someone makes a mistake?

....

....

What are the sacred cows?

....

....

What behaviours are rewarded or punished?

....

....

What happens when someone gives honest feedback?

....

....

What rules or expectations are followed, enforced or ignored?

....

....

Aspired Values
Identify a person who represents your organisation well.

....

....

What is it about him/her that does this?
E.g. good at building relationships/non-judgmental/full of ideas

....

....

Team Exercise

Write down your purpose/mission on a flip chart. Get your team together and ask them these questions:

- What values are essential to us achieving our purpose/mission?
- What is unique about working here?
- What are the principles that form the basis of our decisions?

Take some Post-it notes, and with your leadership team separately write down all the words that come to mind.

Group those together that have roughly the same meaning.

Take the weaker ones away till you have up to five strong values.

Stick them on the wall in the office for a week, to give yourself the time to see if they resonate with you.

Input from external parties

You may wish to invite a group of non-staff members to engage in this exercise e.g. customers, service users, volunteers, trustees. It is likely that you will receive valuable information from their per-spective about your *actual* values.

CHAPTER 5

How (Part 1): Embedding our Values

Felicity was surprised when Nicola asked her to chair the values working group. Nicola had said she had asked her because she embodied the organisation's values.

As Nicola's PA, she did always do the best job she could, took every opportunity to learn new systems of work, spoke up if she felt something was wrong, always in a respectful manner, and encouraged those quieter members of staff to share their ideas.

Embedding our Values

We need our people and our organisations to embody our values for the following reasons:

- *Flow* – our values flow into our operations, producing a consistency of approach and behaviour, bringing alignment in the way our organisation operates.

- *Integrity* – our operations reflect who we are; the experience people have of us is the same as who we declare ourselves to be.

- *Norms* – we create a set of norms that guide our behaviours, creating a culture that has a life and momentum of its own.

- *Loyalty* – in being loyal to our values, we attract the loyalty of our people.

- *Growth* – our organisation naturally grows according to principles that are important to us and how we have defined success.

- *Safety* – it will be the norm to speak up when values are being breached.

- *Business culture* – our business culture reflects our true values.

If values are to be effectively embedded throughout the organisation, every member of the organisation should be involved, engaged. An effective way of doing this is through *a values working group*, which is made up of a cross section of nominated individuals from within the organisation. The detail of how this group would operate is outlined below.

Values working group – aims

- To define the *actual* culture.

- To report back on how the values are being demonstrated and where there is room for improvement.

- To contribute to drafting a set of working practices and creative ways to embed the values.

- To act as champions and channels of communication to the rest of the organisation.

- To give continuous feedback as to how the values are being outworked so they can be talked about and celebrated.

This last point refers to the *story* each organisation has. How do people talk about your organisation from within? Do they speak negatively of certain people, decisions that have been made etc.? Or do they speak well of your leadership, and proudly of challenges or achievements? It's all too easy to focus on challenges, mistakes, and aspects of the organisation that aren't good, but this kind of story really does steal energy and hope.

If, however, we begin to highlight and celebrate how individuals from across the organisation are demonstrating the values, then we will begin to change the focus of the narrative, to an organisation to be proud of. The culture will be moulded into an organisation that celebrates each other. This will then naturally progress to your reputation from those outside the organisation. This exercise will serve as an investment in your public relations.

It's important to emphasise again that the most effective and long-lasting way that culture is shaped is by example. Therefore, alongside the leadership team leading the way (more about this in chapter 7), this group exhibiting their expression of the values will be the most effective way to shape culture in the long run. The case studies towards the end of the chapter give examples of this.

Step 1 – Choose your facilitator

It may sound obvious, but you need to choose someone with facilitation skills, i.e. able to ensure that everyone is involved, tease out ideas, and gather together collected thoughts. They also need to be someone who buys-in to the values and the process. Ideally, like Felicity, find someone who embodies the values.

Alternatively, you could use your own HR person, Training Officer, or an external consultant.

Step 2 – Recruit your cultural ambassadors

Your group should ideally be no more than six people, as diverse as possible, taken from different departments, levels, roles, ages and genders. Diversity is important, as it avoids 'groupthink', that psychological dynamic where those with similar backgrounds and experiences set aside their own beliefs and adopt the opinion of the rest of the group.

Recruit your group with the following criteria:

- They are able to inspire those around them.

- They are observant.

- They are candid, not afraid to give honest feedback.

- They can commit to attending the meetings.

- They are going to engage positively.

During this process, some may find themselves needing to off-load gripes in terms of values not being demonstrated. This should be allowed to happen, but sensitively and skillfully facilitated, in order for the group to move on.

Approach them personally. Tell them that they have been hand-picked for the job because of their ability to think outside the box, work well with others and bring honest and constructive feedback.

Explain the aims (as above) and the requirements on them to:

- Offer up their perspectives, observations and ideas.

- Commit to attending.

- Champion the culture that will emerge.

- Do a little bit of work in between meetings.

In terms of what's in it for them, they have the opportunity to play a key role in the shaping of a workplace culture that is going to make coming to work more enjoyable and fulfilling.

Step 3 – Hold the meetings

Ideally, there should be four meetings two weeks apart with a fifth set as a review meeting, with the following agendas:

MEETING 1

Purpose: to get to know each other, gain understanding of the power of culture and for the facilitator to enthuse them about being involved. Explain the aims (as above) and then go on to describe the meaning of culture and how an organisation's values shape it as follows:

- Culture is made up of the beliefs, traditions, values and norms of behaviour.

- It can often be described as the atmosphere, the way we do things.

- Culture hugely influences your enjoyment and performance at work.

- A positive culture can make your organisation more successful.

We can shape our culture to be one where people feel valued, empowered and motivated by taking the organisation's values and making them real.

Then go on to describe the organisation's values or draft values. Offer up some examples of how your values are outworking already, to get them thinking. Finally give each of them a note-book and pen and send them away to observe how values are being outworked.

In the past, I have made the mistake of enthusiastically calling the last point 'homework'. I soon realised my mistake when I saw how busy the group already were; they didn't need to be burdened by more work. Therefore, I would emphasise that this requirement to observe is incorporated into their everyday work and interactions.

MEETING 2

Purpose: gain feedback, begin to gather words and phrases that describe the values being actioned and start to tell stories. Specifically:

- Take feedback from their observations to get a picture of how the values are being outworked; identify some good examples to tell stories about.

- Break down the values into behaviours, beliefs, attitudes, approaches.

- Identify some behaviours, processes, or actions that aren't aligned to your values. Make a note of these, for the group's attention only, and come up with ideas as to how the group will demonstrate and encourage the opposite behaviours.

- Think of some ways to start telling a new narrative. One way would be that after every meeting send out an 'all staff' email giving examples of how your staff have demonstrated the values (see Chapter 6 for examples).

- Begin to come up with some ways to cascade the values through the organisation e.g. pick some key words or pictures to put on the wall, introduce values on the respective team agendas, print on ID cards etc. or come up with an anagram e.g. Courage, Learning, Empowerment, Authenticity, Respect (CLEAR) or Passion, Excellence, Adventure, Curiosity, Environment (PEACE).

MEETING 3

Purpose: continue to gain feedback and come up with some systems (see chapter 6) that will serve to nurture and maintain this emerging culture.

As in meeting 2, take feedback and send out an email to all staff to celebrate the values being outworked.

Identify ways to embed the values in key processes such as recruitment, formal HR processes, appraisal forms, working practices, marketing, management protocols and in particular those that will maintain the values embedding process (again, see chapter 6).

MEETING 4

Purpose: keep cementing and understanding how the values could be expressed and gain further ideas and commitment to driving the values deeper into the fabric of the organisation.

As in meeting 2, take feedback and send out an email to all staff to celebrate the values being outworked.

Design a short presentation for presenting the values at the next induction day or departmental or whole staff meeting to be delivered by members of the group.

At this stage in the process, everyone in the organisation should be becoming more aware of the values and how to align themselves with them. In order for this not to become just another initiative that fizzles out, systems of working should be put in place at this stage. I will explain more about these and give some examples in chapter 6.

MEETING 5

Three months from the date of meeting 4, hold a further meeting to:

- Review the feedback of the outworking of the values.

- Action anything that is outstanding from ideas in previous meetings.

- Determine how effectively embedding the systems is working and identify ways to maintain the embedding of values.

- Begin to measure the impact of the exercise, by asking the group questions such as: What difference have you observed in your colleagues'/manager's behaviour? Thus far, how has the embedding of the values had an impact on morale/motivation/performance?

A good way to see if this process is working is to ask a random selection of staff to name the organisation's values and state what practical action they could take to uphold them in their day-to-day work.

FURTHER MEETINGS

I would then suggest holding further meetings twice annually with the following aims:

- To review how effective the systems for maintaining the embedding of values are.

- To send out a staff questionnaire asking if they can name the values, give examples of how they are demonstrating them, and give an example of when they have observed their manager's behaviour aligning to them.

Case Study No 1:

The Joseph Rowntree Foundation[22], a social change organisation working to solve poverty in the UK underwent a values embedding process in 2017. Their values were important to them, but few could definitively say what they were. They understood that if their 800-strong workforce were clear on their values and what they meant, the various parts of the organisation would work better together. They didn't want their senior management to choose the values; they wanted to involve their staff at an early stage.

With academics, gardeners, caregivers, and more than five hundred of them having no access to email, involving all the staff was a challenge. They set up their 'values champion steering group' from different areas of the workforce, starting with a survey and a series of workshops to gather stories from their staff about how they do things.

They then distilled the information into eight shortlisted areas and asked each employee to choose their favourite three. Those employees not on email weren't left out; buckets and tokens were taken into care homes, to enable those staff to cast their votes.

At the end of the process, JRF had nailed down its three core values:

We show we care – We make a difference – We are built on trust

By way of embedding their values, they use them in internal appraisals and recruitment processes, ensuring that they recruit people who share their values, understanding that skills can be taught and developed, but values can't.

A second staff survey at the end of the process revealed that 95 per cent knew what the organisation's values were.

Case Study No 2:

Eastbourne and Wealden YMCA[23] is a medium-sized charity, of around fifty staff supporting vulnerable young people to live independently. Ideas for values were discussed at the senior management team level. At the end of the process, they decided on five: Honour, Generosity, Acceptance, Authenticity and Courage.

The team handpicked their cultural ambassadors and set about breaking down their values into a set of attitudes, beliefs and behaviours. They then followed the five-stage meeting process outlined in this chapter. Following their recommendations, the values were written into one-to-one reviews and the recruitment process, and used to design management training and deliver staff development programmes.

In referring to the culture that resulted, the charity's CEO said: 'The blame culture has been replaced by a let's address it together culture.'

Conclusion

Embedding values takes intentionality and patience because you are asking people to dedicate time out of their already busy lives to think creatively.

You can't shortcut this process. Actively engaging your staff will take more time than if you brought your senior management team together and between you decided on some behaviours for everyone to follow. However, following a process such as the one outlined in this chapter is more likely to ensure that your people will *choose* to align their behaviours to the organisation's values.

Summary

- ☐ If our people embody our values the organisation will produce and deliver its services according to our principles, in an integral way.

- ☐ An effective way of engaging with all of our staff is through a values working group who meet regularly (recommended four meetings).

- ☐ The values working group should come up with ways to outwork the values, begin to tell stories about good practice and act as cultural ambassadors for the culture-shape process.

- ☐ A fifth meeting can be held three months from the date of meeting 4, to review how effectively the values are being embedded.

- ☐ The values working group should then meet twice yearly to review the process.

Action Checklist 4

List the aims of the values working group (take from this chapter or add your own).

....

....

Name some suggested facilitators.

....

....

Name your values working group members.

....

....

List the venue and date of your first meeting.

....

....

How does *your* behaviour reflect your personal values?

....

....

CHAPTER 6

How (Part 2): Six Ways to Embed our Values

Andy, the HR Manager, reflected on how many times he saw undesirable behaviour that fell outside the organisation's policies and procedures.

For example, when James came into the office in a mood, usually when his football team had lost, it would be like 'walking on eggshells' around him. Or when Jacqui was at the photocopier, she would have another moan about her line manager's decisions. And Phil, clearly showing favouritism, would pick out certain members of staff to thank for work done. Individuals would come to Andy and complain, but he couldn't seem to pinpoint the issues onto any particular policy.

He realised that you could still have a negative culture, even if all policies were being adhered to.

With the introduction of the values embedding process, however, in which all staff were expected to demonstrate the values in their roles, he felt hopeful that this could be the door to addressing these tricky issues. For his part, he set about reviewing the HR policies to see how the values influenced *how* the policies were implemented.

Six Ways to Embed our Values

Shaping a positive culture takes intentionality, perseverance and time because, as we know, culture doesn't change overnight. To sustain a change in culture, working practices need to be revised to reflect the organisation's values. Here are six processes that will help you do this:

1.Staff review forms – reaching everyone

Adding a values question to the staff review process is a good way to reach the whole organisation. You can do this by taking a value, and inviting the individual to identify a specific action to demonstrate the value. For example:

Value: Accountability

Annie gets angry or hurt when receiving criticism.

> *'When someone gives me feedback, I will thank them,
> ask myself if there is any truth to it, and discard the rest.'*

Value: Courage

Jack hates making presentations but knows that he needs to become more confident in this skill if he is going to progress through the organisation.

> *'I will offer to deliver the team update at the next
> staff meeting (practicing with a colleague beforehand).'*

Value: Authenticity

Sean talks too much and tends to dominate meetings.

> *'I will ask my staff team to raise their water bottle/coffee
> cup if I am interrupting or talking too much.'*

Value: Creativity

Raj tends to come to his manager when there is a problem, rather than thinking of a creative solution himself.

> *'When I see a problem, I will ask myself what a solution could be e.g. if the reception area is too cramped, I will suggest and help to rearrange the room.'*

2.Recruitment – choosing well from the outset

It is much easier to train someone to become proficient in something than it is to teach someone to take on an attitude, approach or belief.

The surveys outlined in *Good to Great*[24] by Jim Collins found that the great companies hired people for their character attributes such as work ethic, dedication to fulfilling commitments, and values, before education, work experience, skills and knowledge. The latter list, they realised, could be taught, the former was much harder to train people in, if at all.

If you have a member of staff who isn't empowering (see example 2) they may not see the need to empower others or they may be overly focused on themselves; in this case, their team will not grow.

If you have a member of staff who is judgmental, (see example 2) or has an attitude of moral superiority, this is likely to be discerned by the service user who may then withdraw.

In 2013, Google carried out a study[25] on their hiring, firing and promotion data since their incorporation in 1998. The company used to hire according to the top-grade students from elite science universities, favouring the STEM subjects (science, technology, engineering, mathematics). In the study they analysed the most important eight qualities (later updated to ten) of their top employees. They found that the seven top characteristics of success at Google are soft skills that are effectively creating a culture in which people are empowered to do their best. Technical skills came in at number eight.

It is therefore worth spending time designing a selection process to ensure that you recruit the right people from the outset. At this early stage, you take a value that is particularly important in that role and ask the interviewee how they will demonstrate it, if they are successful in getting the job. Here are some examples of how this might work:

Example 1

Role: Manager

Value: Empowerment

Question: What tools will you use to ensure that each member of your team is empowered? Give an example of how this would work.

Possible answer: make a point of finding out their strengths and aspirations.

E.g. the receptionist organises charity events at her local badminton group. Ask her to plan a charity event to promote community involvement and raise the profile of the organisation.

Exercise: ask your interviewee to choose three strengths out of a list of ten, and give ideas as to how they could empower their team to build on each of the strengths.

Example 2

Role: Housing Support Worker

Value: Acceptance

Question: How are you going to demonstrate an accepting/non-judgmental approach to some of our service users, e.g. substance misusers?

Possible answer: take the belief that it could have been me in that situation, or recognise that everyone has intrinsic value.

Example exercise: design a simple poster with words and/or images welcoming people as they enter the premises.

I would suggest that the values working group devises a list of potential questions to test the outworking of each of the values. You may want to bring in a member of HR to facilitate this exercise.

Developing a more inclusive culture: unconscious bias

Increasingly companies are introducing ways to address unconscious bias – the phenomena where personal experiences, societal stereotypes and cultural context can have an impact on your decisions and actions without realising it. Methods include training in the science of unconscious bias, common biases and how these biases negatively affect decisions, as well as providing checklists as to how to avoid them.

3.Formal HR processes – weaving in compassion and dignity

When someone comes into the workplace, you may not know or see what they are experiencing outside of the workplace in their personal lives.

Sometimes people are coping with physical illness, depression, relationship breakdowns, financial hardship; in fact, situations that we are all likely to experience at some point in our lives. These situations sometimes affect our work. Of course, if it was us, we would want to be treated in a sympathetic and respectful way.

There needs to be a fairness and consistency in how we deal with staff issues; our policies are designed to provide this. However, they can take precedence above the spirit of an organisation that places great value on its people.

When we are faced with someone whose conduct or capability is less than satisfactory, it is frustrating, and the temptation can be to deal with the individual in a less than respectful manner.

I would suggest that the HR lead thinks of some specific ways that the formal HR processes should operate, according to your values. For example, training your managers in qualities key to creating a positive culture e.g. communication, emotional intelligence, empowerment (see chapter 7).

If the decision is made to terminate an employee's contract, how you treat the individual who leaves the organisation is as important as how you treat those who stay. And, of course, they are more likely to speak positively about you to their family, friends and acquaintances.

4. Management protocols – guidance for managers

An effective way of ensuring your values are woven into your management practices (again, more about the key role of managers and leaders in shaping culture in Chapter 7) is through a series of protocols.

Meetings can be a window into an organisation's culture. You can learn a lot about an organisation's actual culture by observing relationship dynamics, how comfortable people are sharing their ideas, the level of freedom to challenge one other, and what happens when someone dominates the meeting. Meetings can reveal who holds the power, and how much individuals are valued.

Task your management team with putting these protocols together, starting with how the organisation is going to run their meetings according to their values. For example:

Values: respect, individuality, collaboration, learning, excellence.

Management Protocols - Meetings

We will:

- Start and finish on time.

- Send the agenda items out at least two days before the meeting.

- Time the agenda items and stick to the timings.

- Allow everyone around the table to contribute.

- Seek first to understand others' positions before we give our opinion.

- Refrain from interruption.

- Seek to find ways to work together to find solutions.

- Ensure we clearly articulate outcomes and action points.

Management Protocols – Communication

We will:

- Ensure our emails are as concise as possible.

- Reflect our organisation's culture in all communication, not using these opportunities to push our own agendas.

- Ensure communications are very well prepared.

- Call or speak to someone in person if they have upset us; we don't fire off an email or find someone to complain to.

- If we notice a performance problem with one of our staff, quickly take the initiative and go and speak to them in private.

- Follow up after the meeting to ensure that the actions have taken place.

Management Protocols – Decision-making

We will:

- Obtain counsel from one or two trusted colleagues, when making important decisions.

- Seek feedback as to the quality of our decision-making.

- Set timescales and keep them; be accountable to others if we tend to procrastinate.

- Always ensure we have sought to perceive all angles of a tricky situation before we make a decision.

5. Shape your story

An organisation's story is what both employees and observers say about the organisation; they should make your values come alive. An organisation will, through their website, media and their branding, present an image of themselves that may or may not be the true image.

Those who are best placed to comment on whether the image the organisation presents is the true image are the employees.

As we saw in Chapter 1, if the presented image is not the true image, then there is disconnect between what an organisation says it is, and what it actually is. When we identify our values and work hard to embed them into the organisation we create alignment between the two. An important part of the embedding process is to nurture a narrative within the organisation.

When you and your employees talk positively about your culture, this reinforces it. If you have gone through the stages already set out in this book, to a certain extent, that should be happening automatically. In order for people to be able to celebrate values being demonstrated outside of their immediate vicinity, there needs to be an information channel.

Here are some ideas:

Make a film

Brightec[26], the mobile app agency mentioned in chapter 4, have made a film to demonstrate their culture. This serves not only to build pride with existing staff but is also attractive to potential clients and employees. See **www.brightec.com**.

Add 'stories' to your regular team meetings

Finding and verbalising good stories that people have about working for you will act as a bridge between where you are and what you aspire to be. Getting into the habit of telling such stories will help you to create and grow a positive and healthy culture.

Write a newsletter

Collate examples of people demonstrating the organisation's values. The values working group can start this process (see chapter 5, values working group, step 3). I would suggest the group's facilitator send out a fortnightly newsletter and after three or four months, reduce this to one every month or two.

Example newsletter

We understand that creating a positive work culture will enable us all to grow, to use our talents to be more productive, and to be more fulfilled at work. Values underpin our culture and in order to keep strengthening it we need to be demonstrating them in our respective roles. This is our fortnightly newsletter containing some examples of how we express our values. Look out for our values being demonstrated and send them to Sally in the Admin office.

'Having been rushed into hospital for an emergency operation, I awoke to find a beautiful card and the biggest bunch of flowers from my team!'

Jane.

'Having taken over the service, and in the midst of challenging competition, Nicky has managed to turn a deficit into a healthy profit within nine months.'

James (Nicky's manager).

'In a recent management team meeting, we had a particularly tricky issue to solve. There was a lively discussion at the end of which a decision was made. The team member that wouldn't have chosen that decision chose to support the final decision in their allegiance to the overall team.'

Jimmy (newly recruited manager).

'My teammates knew I was nervous about the presentation. During the morning before I was to get up and speak, I received no less than six texts from colleagues encouraging me; this gave me the confidence to carry me through my talk.'

Grant.

VALUES: GENEROSITY/INNOVATION/RESPECT/ ENCOURAGEMENT

This process reveals to employees that they aren't just carrying out their jobs, but they are influencing their team and the whole organisation. You are helping them to understand that they are part of a bigger group of people. In doing so, you are providing a sense of meaning to the roles within the workplace.

6 Induction

The induction is your opportunity to introduce new staff to your values and the resulting culture in order that they are enthused about your organisational culture at the outset.

Here's an idea of how you could build in a values slot to your induction event:

> To begin with, ask the group to introduce themselves, with each person giving their first impressions of the organisation. This will be helpful feedback for you in terms of how well your values are being reflected.
>
> Get one or several members of the values working group to briefly explain each of your values and give an example of how they express each one in their roles.
>
> **And then either:**
>
> Ask the group to spend five minutes noting down how they will demonstrate each of the values in their roles, feeding back to the whole group with their suggestions.
>
> **Or:**
>
> Stick some flip chart paper on the wall with a value heading on each one. Get the group to go round with coloured pens and write beneath each one a word or phrase to describe how they would express that value.

The aim of these exercises would be to communicate, at the outset, that all staff, even brand new ones, have a role to fulfil in contributing to the values being expressed and the resultant culture.

Conclusion

The day-to-day process of embedding values can be tiresome and is therefore often the stage in shaping culture that is missed out. However, whilst the behaviour that results from adhering to a set of policies does contribute to a workplace culture, it is these embedding processes that create a culture that is long-lasting. This chapter has hopefully given you some ideas.

Summary

- ☐ Even if all policies are being adhered to, a negative culture can still exist because norms of behaviour often fall outside of rules that are written down.

- ☐ An effective way of embedding values is to set up some systems in which you can feed in your values. Here are some examples:

  - *Staff review forms* – add a question asking how the individual would demonstrate a particular value.

  - *Recruitment* – relate a value to an aspect of the role and ask how the interviewee would demonstrate or has demonstrated it.

  - *HR processes* – ensure policies, and how they are handled, align to your values.

  - *Management protocols* – give guidelines on how your management practices are conducted.

  - *Shaping your story* – finding and verbalising positive accounts of the demonstration of your values will reinforce your culture.

  - *Induction* – asking individuals to give examples of how they demonstrate the organisation's values will communicate expectations right at the beginning of employment.

Action Checklist 5

Think of a value and design a question for someone stepping into your role.

....

....

List three Management Protocols that you would like to create.

....

....

What is the last thing you heard from someone talking about your organisation from within/without?

....

....

What would you like someone external to the organisation to say about it?

....

....

What do you need to do in order for this to occur?

....

....

Which is the easiest process for you to adopt of the six outlined here? Which is the hardest?

....

....

CHAPTER 7

Who: Equipping Managers: Seven
Qualities of a Culture-Shaping Leader

*The main reason that Future Kids Project Co-ordinator Billy
left his previous job was the behaviour of Geoff, his line
manager. He lacked the following character traits:*

Resilience – during times of challenge, Geoff would
disappear, often taking a day's absence if there was a key
meeting happening. This left the team feeling insecure and
unsupported.

Empowerment – Geoff didn't seem interested in what
Billy enjoyed most about his role, or about his aspirations.
This resulted in Billy having few opportunities to develop,
and missing out on a promotion opportunity he knew he
had the potential for.

Emotional intelligence – Geoff prided himself on being
emotionally intelligent. Unfortunately, his team experienced
him as grumpy and self-centred. They were left feeling
unvalued, unimportant, and not listened to.

Decision-making – Geoff's reluctance to take
responsibility for his decisions meant that he would blame
everyone else if he made a wrong decision. Consequently,
the team had lost confidence in him and were making
decisions without consulting him.

Communication – Geoff avoided addressing behavioural
or poor performance situations, as he was intimidated by
one or two prickly members of the team. The outcome was

manipulation and mild bullying by some individuals of others.

Vision – Geoff didn't show any enthusiasm about the organisation's future, failing to communicate direction and goals to the team. For this reason, the team was unfocused and unmotivated.

Courage – Geoff lacked a quality that was needed to master all of the above qualities, evident in his unwillingness to admit that he was occasionally in the wrong: courage. His insistence that he was always right made him unlikeable and eventually lost him Billy's respect.

Who: Equipping Managers

As we know, it's the leaders who set cultures within organisations, to a positive or negative effect. If a leader allows people autonomy in *how* they complete their roles they will create a culture of trust and flexibility. Individuals are then motivated to come up with new ideas, go the extra mile and take accountability for their work. Alternatively, the leader who keeps a tight control on how roles are carried out shuts down creativity; this can result in a culture that is to do the very minimum and no more.

What follows in this chapter, are the outlines of seven qualities that I have observed over the years as being crucial to creating a positive culture. If you are a CEO, have people who report to you, or are in a position of responsibility, these leadership qualities are essential. Each of the following sections gives:

- An outline of each quality

- Its impact on workplace culture

- Ways to develop the quality

Appendix A consists of a questionnaire on each quality that I would suggest you do by way of a self-assessment before you read the chapter. You can address this chapter in two ways:

- Take yourself and your team through one quality every month.

- Use it as a basis to develop your own leadership programme.

Seven Leadership Qualities

I happen to be one of those million women in the UK that regularly run. I was running up a long hill recently, and watching a more experienced runner up ahead; she was the inspiration I needed to keep my tired legs going. Towards the top, she stopped and, oddly, so did I. I gave myself permission to stop because she had. If she couldn't reach the top, I told myself, it was unlikely that I could.

As leaders, we have an immense impact through our decisions and actions on those around us. And when we face challenges and setbacks, it's especially important that we don't give up. The first quality is *resilience*.

Quality 1: RESILIENCE

Definition: to have an emotional robustness and to be able to bounce back after setbacks.

Words that describe resilience: confidence, determination, persistence, inner strength, emotional robustness, transparency, buoyancy.

NB Notice that being resilient doesn't mean that you don't get knocked back; it means that you have the capacity to get back up on your feet again.

Why is resilience important?

In the workplace, we are expected to handle a huge amount of pressure, a heavy workload and responsibility, amidst a climate of uncertainty. With today's culture of instant credit, 24/7 access to entertainment, and to friends and acquaintances, via social media, the danger is that we don't learn to endure difficulty or to have to wait for something. Younger people have a natural disadvantage, as resilience comes with age. Life experience proves to us that even when bad things happen e.g. disappointments, setbacks, delays, heartbreak, we can usually survive them.

It's against a backdrop of instant gratification that leaders are required to calmly carry on and not give up.

The culture that a resilient leader grows around him/her is as follows:

Safety
They are emotionally strong and calm in a crisis. This will lead to the team being able to get on with their jobs, in a culture that is free from anxiety, in the knowledge that their manager will shoulder those challenges.

Well-being
They can manage their stress, know their triggers, know how to recharge, and are less likely to take sickness absence or buckle during times of extreme pressure. They are open about their need to take care of themselves. This will result in a culture where well-being is discussed and valued.

Solution-focused
When change or setbacks occur, they are adaptable. Instead of being overwhelmed by the circumstances, they are able to bring solutions, a way forward. This will result in a culture where creative problem solving is encouraged.

Hope
They stay positive but realistic; they don't have their heads in the sand. They take the approach that 'every cloud has a silver lining'. This creates a culture where people can feel hopeful in every situation.

One way to develop resilience: know your values.

If you can connect with your values, you can find meaning in everything you experience.

A friend of mine has a value of *learning*; he reads a book a week feeding his need to continuously learn, which his day-to-day job simply cannot do. He then takes it a step further. He shares his learning by sending out a summary of each book to a group of people who also love to learn, but don't have a similar mental capacity.

One of my values is *uniqueness*; I believe that we are all one-offs and that we have a unique contribution to make to the world. Observing talented people whose talents remained dormant eventually prompted me to leave my job and start a consultancy to help businesses create the working conditions where talents are untapped, benefiting both employees and the business. Recognising this value has given my working life meaning, as I'm hopefully making a difference to people who would otherwise feel unimportant and unvalued; it has also kept me moving forward in the unpredictable world of self-employment.

When you reflect on your values, the story you tell yourself about stress shifts. You become more likely to approach challenges rather than avoid them and you are better able to see the meaning in difficult circumstances.

Try this:
Take ten minutes to write about your values. List four values and state how you are demonstrating them in your life. Name two things you could do tomorrow that would demonstrate them further.

Some other ways to develop resilience

Understand what you can and can't control: identify a stressful situation and draw up three lists. The first being those things you can control, the second those things you can't control but can influence, and the third, those things you can't control. Discard the latter list. It's pointless being anxious about something you can do nothing about.

Practice thankfulness: list ten things that you are thankful for. Research suggests that adults, who keep gratitude journals on a regular basis, report fewer illness symptoms, feel better about their lives as a whole and are more optimistic about the future.

Grow a social support network: studies have shown that having social support reduces stress and brings longevity. It seems to be particularly important that men make time for finding support amongst others.

Build in time to recharge: find out what activities, situations and people energise you and carve out time to do those things or mix with those people.

Quality 2: EMPOWERMENT

Definition: to identify potential talent and to encourage and give people opportunity to develop.

Words/phrases that describe empowerment: trust, take a risk with someone, delegate and allow autonomy, value diversity.

Why is it important to be empowering?

Learning to empower others will result in people growing in aptitude, confidence and expertise. It's essential for the organisation to keep moving forward in achieving its mission. If a talented individual isn't empowered, they won't develop into their potential, and they may seek to join a team in which they *will* have opportunities to grow.

The culture that an empowering leader grows around them is:

Strengths-focused

The empowering leader's team knows values and brings to the surface each other's strengths. Less time is spent on putting performance plans in place to try to make that individual 'well-rounded' and more time is spent giving them opportunities to use their natural talents.

'Can-do'

Individuals in the team develop, spurring each other on as they encourage one another to stretch themselves and take risks.

No blame

Mistakes are expected, if individuals and the team are to move forward e.g. new ways of doing things are tried, or new ideas followed through that don't end up working. The team performs better.

Trust

There is a culture of trust as the team members know that they can experiment and try something new because their jobs are secure.

Diversity

As a leader you understand that different perspectives and approaches bring great value to the team; coming from a different background or culture is welcomed.

One way to become more empowering: become a talent spotter.

Sometimes talent is left dormant, because the team leader is threatened by their potential, maybe due to a lack of self-esteem within themselves. One way to remedy this is to recognise what your own talents are.

Try this:

From the strengths chart below identify three words that you can identify as your own strengths and two strengths for two of your team members. Make a point to tell each of those people what you think their strengths are in the next week.

Good communicator	Strategic thinker	Visionary
Spotter of potential	Solution finder	Empathetic
Sense of humour	Creative	Organised
Able to concentrate well	Initiator	Good networker
Decision-maker	Finisher	Includer
Attention to detail	Quick learner	Encourager
Problem solver	Listener	Empowerer
Good at project management	Adaptable	Courageous

Here are some other ways to become more empowering:

Find out what your employee's aspirations are: ask them what they would really love to do. You will begin to see a bigger picture and may start to identify some transferable skills.

Do some more in-depth work around strengths: a reputable, well-regarded profile model should help the team members understand their individual strengths and appreciate and call upon those of their colleagues.

Ask questions: instead of offering up your solutions, use a coaching approach e.g. ask them 'What are your options?' or 'What are three things you could do to move the situation forward?' prompting them to find answers themselves.

Delegate something out of the individual's comfort zone: make sure you give them the resources to achieve the assignment, give clarity on the outcome and timescale, but allow them to decide how they are going to achieve the task.

Quality 3: EMOTIONAL INTELLIGENCE

Definition: to be able to understand and manage your emotions, and be sensitive to the emotions of those around you.

Words/phrases that describe emotional intelligence: awareness, empathy, calmness, honesty, humility, social skills, understanding.

NB In this description, I am including both self and social awareness.

Why it is important to be emotionally intelligent?

An emotionally intelligent leader will know what their team thinks of them. This is important because you won't develop yourself if you aren't open to hearing feedback from others. Understanding yourself will help to begin to understand others, and you will be able to steer behaviour, ensuring those with the strongest emotions don't dominate to the detriment of the team.

The culture that an empowering leader grows around them:

No taboos

If people know that giving honest feedback, in a respectful way, won't put their job at risk, then a culture of transparency will emerge. There will be no room for issues to be 'swept under the carpet'.

No gossip

The expectation is, when problems arise, individuals go and speak directly to each other. Gossip becomes unacceptable.

Humility

Opening ourselves up to feedback demonstrates that we all have strengths and weaknesses. Those with large egos won't survive in this environment.

Continuous learning

The resistance to change because 'we've always done things this way' will be challenged. Team performance is bound to improve. This will result in a culture where everyone is expected to keep learning.

One way to become more emotionally intelligent is to know yourself.

Try this reflection exercise:

Look back at the last 24 hours and note down each time a situation or a person triggered strong emotion in you. Ask yourself where this emotion comes from. Does being asked to clarify the reasons behind a decision make me feel insecure in my position? Does this person who dominates the conversation contravene my value of listening? Link some action points to these e.g. remind myself that being honest about my weaknesses generates respect from the team, give feedback to the 'talker' that their behaviour is stopping others' contributions.

Some more ways to develop your emotional intelligence:

Find an outlet to get in touch with your emotions: e.g. journaling, playing music, watching a film, drawing, or painting.

Be aware of your body language: when someone is talking to you give them your full attention, don't fidget or interrupt, and keep contact. Ask them for feedback.

Learn to take honest feedback to conquer oversensitivity: ask a trusted friend or family member to give you feedback on one thing you could do to help your relationship. Ask yourself what aspects of the feedback are true, and what you can discard.

Count to ten: if you find yourself about to react with strong emotions, this can help you to calm down and reconnect with your ability to be objective.

Quality 4: DECISION-MAKING

Definition: to make timely and considered decisions, by identifying the options, foreseeing consequences, and then taking responsibility for the outcome.

Words/phrases that describe a good decision maker: quick, confident, brave, logical, considerate of and open to advice from others.

Why is it important to be able to make good decisions?

If you are a leader, the ability to make good decisions is crucial. Whether it's working as a doctor in A&E where you need to make quick decisions, confidently and calmly, or you are a team leader and need to make day-to-day decisions that are timely, rational and workable to maintain the trust and respect of your team.

The culture that a good decision maker grows around them:

Trust

As a leader gains a track record of making predominantly good decisions, they will gain the respect and trust of the team providing them with the security to make their own decisions.

Mistakes happen

If leaders set the example of using their wrong decisions (that they will inevitably make) as learning opportunities, that aren't hidden, the team will grow in confidence in their decision making without fearing a detriment to their job if they make a mistake.

Accountability

If the leader is taking responsibility for the outcome of decisions made, then this will create a culture of accountability, where it is expected that you answer for your decisions, thus avoiding a blame culture.

Security

The knowledge that the person responsible for making decisions can be trusted to make them, gives a feeling of security to the team, allowing them to get on with their jobs.

One way to improve your decision-making skills: consider the process.

Often wrong decisions are made because we haven't followed through a step-by-step process.

Try this seven-step decision-making process:

1 Identify a problem or opportunity

2 Gather information

3 Identify the alternatives

4 Weigh up each alternative

5 Choose from the alternatives

6 Take action

7 Evaluate the results

Some more ways to become a better decision maker:

Be accountable to someone else: particularly with deadlines if you tend to procrastinate.

Be independent: if you tend to only make decisions with others, you may flounder when you are called to make a quick decision by yourself. Before you ask others advice, trust your own decision making.

Stop seeking perfection: all that is expected of you is that you make the best decision you can with the information you have available at the time. Take the risk of getting it wrong occasionally.

Sleep on it: giving yourself time takes you out of the immediate emotions of a tough decision and enables you to take a more objective approach.

Quality 5: COMMUNICATION

Definition: to listen well and be able to express your ideas, opinions and wishes concisely with open body language, and not shying away from difficult conversations.

Words/phrases that describe a good communicator: brave, listens, respectful of others opinions, confident, considered.

Why it is important to be able to be a good communicator?

Leaders that communicate well usually have a high performing team. There is little ambiguity over expectations so the team know what they need to do and feedback on performance is specific, not vague. There is a transparency within the team as honest feedback is welcome.

The culture that a good communicator grows around them:

High performing

Expectations around tasks and timescales are clearly communicated.

No 'elephants in the room'

Awkward behavioural traits or inappropriate language or behaviour cannot remain in this culture as the leader is quick to address them; thus setting a transparent culture.

Performance issues nipped in the bud

The leader is quick to address unsatisfactory performance and isn't afraid of confronting damaging attitudes or difficult situations such as personality clashes, not allowing them to develop into bigger issues.

No gossip

The practice is that issues are dealt with face-to-face, avoiding tittle-tattle at the coffee machine.

One way to improve your ability to communicate: practice giving specific feedback.

Try this:

In your review process with the individuals in your team whether that's one-to-one, or peer group, annual, monthly or spontaneous, include some feedback questions, such as:

Ask them which strengths they have demonstrated well this year and then follow up by giving your feedback. This would require you to have an understanding of their strengths (again, there are several models on the market, but I've found Gallup Strengthsfinder particularly good).

Tell them what else they have done particularly well this year. It could be:

- How well they resolved a particular problem or the way they resolved it

- That they've made a good decision

- That they've completed a piece of work well

- That they supported or inspired you in some way.

Finish this sentence: one thing they could do by way of an improvement would be:

Some more ways to become a better communicator:

Check your approachability: ask someone who will give you honest feedback.

When addressing a problem with someone seek first to listen and understand: e.g. 'This is my perception of the situation; what is yours?'

Review your style of verbal and written communication: do I ramble at meetings? And are my emails concise?

Get comfortable with silence: some people need time to think for a bit before they respond to a question.

NB An understanding of **extroversion** and **introversion** is essential particularly in terms of communication. Knowing where you are on the E/I scale, and how that has a bearing on how you and others communicate, will improve your communication with others enormously. If you are unfamiliar with the material on extroversion and introversion, there's a variety of questionnaires that can be accessed.[27][28]

Quality 6: VISIONARY

Definition: To imagine your team/organisation and service/product as bigger, better, and stronger and to see where this fits with the external environment. To drive others forward towards this vision.

Words/phrases that describe being visionary: positivity, hope, inventive, innovative, imaginative, insightful, dreamer, strategic.

Why it is important to be visionary?

Leaders must have a vision and strategy, and communicate it to move the organisation forward and to enable people to align themselves towards a shared goal. Individuals know what they are meant to do, and understand why they are doing it. People need to see what is possible. A visionary leader keeps their focus on the vision which motivates them to overcome the inevitable hurdles.

The culture a visionary leader grows around them:

Creativity

In this culture, you have permission to suggest creative solutions to problems, fresh approaches to processes, and innovative ideas regarding services and products.

Autonomy

People are trusted to get on with their jobs; flexible working supports this.

Enthusiasm

The visionary leader's team is enthusiastic about the future. There is a team attitude that there is nothing to lose and a team cohesion that says 'we are all in this together'.

Positivity

This culture fuels a desire not to give up when thing go wrong but to persist in finding a solution seeing problems as opportunities to find a creative solution.

One way to become more visionary: exercise your imagination.

Try this:

Every day for a week, identify a societal problem e.g. the housing crisis, or unemployment, or the decreasing level of natural resources to sustain humankind. Now come up with some outlandish ideas to solve the problem. This should exercise your imagination so that you can begin to apply it to some challenges or problems in your business/life.

Some more ways to become more visionary:

Take yourself away from the immediate situation: you will be able to see things from a different perspective.

Gain inspiration from others: learn everything you can about your organisation, similar organisations and industry.

Read up about a visionary who you admire: they are bound to inspire you.

Reflect and dream about your future: what would you do if you won £5 million?

Quality 7: COURAGE

Definition: to have the mental and moral strength to not allow fear to be a deterrent in taking on a new venture, facing a challenge head-on, or persisting in difficulty.

Words that describe courage: guts, daring, audacity, nerve, grit, spirit, dauntlessness, intrepidity.

Why is courage important?

We need the courage to make decisions, particularly those that could make us unpopular, to initiate new ventures, to keep going when challenges arise, to own up when we are wrong, to recruit a team that is different to us, to have awkward conversations etc. Courage is the foundational quality needed in order for all the other qualities to function well.

The culture that a courageous leader grows around him/ her is as follows:

Initiative

They don't let fear of the unknown stop them from starting new ventures or projects, thereby giving the team permission to do the same. This creates a culture of enthusiasm and excitement about the future.

They don't give up easily

If things don't go to plan, or hurdles appear, they ride the challenges. This creates a culture of adventure and belonging; they are all in it together.

Celebrating difference

They choose to employ a team who are different to them, in views, as well as background, gender, race etc. They don't want a team of yes-men. They understand they will learn more by surrounding themselves by people of different perspectives. This creates a culture of respectful challenge and appreciation of each other.

Authenticity

They are open about their own failings and weaknesses, including when they have been wrong in their views. This creates a culture of openness and transparency.

One way to develop courage: learn a new skill.

Try this:

Learn a new skill, particularly in something you have previously been scared to do. For example, taking an art or dance class, learning a musical instrument or doing a car maintenance workshop, is an excellent way to bring you face-to-face with your lack of knowledge or skill. As you develop your skill, your confidence will develop.

Some other ways to develop courage:

Spend some time with someone who is courageous: e.g. someone who has started their own business, a marathon runner, someone who is living with a terminal illness, or a parent with a child with special needs. I guarantee you will come away inspired and energised.

Identify a life goal and hire a coach to work through it with you: a coach will help you identify your own goals and deadlines, and being accountable to them will mean that you will move forward.

Be transparent to your colleagues/team/partner: they will already know your weaknesses, so it will open up the opportunity for you to grow.

Have a brave conversation: ask your colleagues for honest constructive feedback on something you could improve upon.

Conclusion

If you want to create an environment – or culture – where great things happen, it's worth investing in training your managers. And this is a way, with a minimal investment but intention and commitment, that you can create a healthy culture. These are qualities that may come more easily to some of us, than others. However, I believe that with a good dose of humility, they all can be learned.

Summary

- [ ] Use the self-assessment questionnaire in Appendix A to determine your own leadership qualities.

- [ ] The behaviour and attitude of those in leadership have the most influence in setting a culture.

- [ ] There are particular qualities that can significantly impact a workplace culture; here are seven that I have identified as key:

  - Resilience

  - Empowerment

  - Emotional intelligence

  - Decision-making

  - Communication

  - Vision

  - Courage

- [ ] Some may prove hard to grow in for some, but with an approach of humility, and some time investment, all can be developed or improved upon.

- [ ] You could address this chapter in two ways:

  - Take yourself and your team through one quality every month.

  - Use it as a basis to develop your own leadership programme.

CHAPTER 8
Five Common Traps

Here are some of the mistakes that I have made, observed or experienced.

1 We hold a big launch... and it's received with weariness and cynicism

We draft a set of values amongst our senior team and we go some way towards embedding them. We then hold an event to launch the new values, maybe even complete with T-shirts and prizes. If the process hasn't had the time to bring out some real changes in behaviour and attitudes amongst senior staff, then we may well find that the response will be one of *management initiative weariness.*

Most of us hate change at the best of times, especially when we don't understand the reason for it. An event, promoting a management initiative, that people know little about and don't see the point of, could be viewed as another way for the organisation to try to get more out of their staff. If other initiatives have been launched with little or no follow-up, then we will be met with cynicism. (If you work for an institution that is subject to policies from changes in government, then you will be particularly familiar with this scenario.)

I believe that a gradual introduction to the values and embedding process is more effective than holding a launch, unless it takes place when the process has shown to be making a difference, in which case people will notice that there is a real change in behaviour and attitudes around them. This is why it's particularly important for leaders to make the changes first. It's key that we don't rush the process of culture shaping; we need to trust the process and be patient.

Ways to avoid this: carry out a survey to measure to what extent your values are changing behaviour. If there is evidence that the values are changing behaviour *amongst management*, then hold a launch.

2 Leaders don't live the values

If we as leaders don't think we need to be part of the process that aligns behaviour to values, then we have a problem. It may be that we lack an understanding of the purpose, or we assume that it's other people, not us, who need to change their behaviour. However, even if we think we fully embrace the values, we still need to examine our behaviour in light of the values. We don't want to end up with a 'do as I say not as I do' scenario. This would be more damaging than introducing values in the first place.

Ways to avoid this: Spend at least the first two months of your timetable concentrating on senior managers' behaviours becoming aligned to your values, before you then roll out to non-management staff.

3 We don't involve non-management staff

It's usually easier and quicker to make our decisions amongst peers. It saves time and effort, but sometimes it's counterproductive. The key to this process working is to win the hearts and minds of our employees so that they choose to behave in a way that reflects our values. We are asking people to find their own ways of behaving that demonstrate our values. They need space and time to do so.

Ways to avoid this: set up the values working group as soon as you decide to go down this culture-shaping process, and decide among the senior team that you are going to genuinely listen to their feedback and views, and, as much as you can, act on their feedback.

4 We expect quick financial results

If we want our organisations to be successful, we do need to make the most of our resources. But expecting to see a quick financial gain may impact upon how authentically we follow the process. My culture-shaping method is designed to give everyone the autonomy to influence their own behaviour. In doing so, they will feel valued. However, this may take time. The good news is that staff who feel valued will work harder and are more likely to stay.

Ways to avoid this: decide to see success through the lens of change in behaviour, at least for the duration of this process.

5 Our culture becomes exclusive

This is possibly the most important trap to be aware of. It's natural to gravitate towards those who are like us. If you have ever been abroad and encountered someone who is from your home country, all of sudden you sense a connection. Someone with whom you wouldn't normally connect with, back home, you have something in common with.

We do need to be careful that we don't allow our culture to become exclusive. There is a difference between not recruiting someone because they don't share our organisational values or because 'their face doesn't fit'; they don't look like, sound like or, for example, have had the same kind of education as us.

Unfortunately, some organisations use the culture argument to exclude others, unlawfully or just wrongly.

Having a values-driven culture does create boundaries in terms of the behaviours and attitudes that grow from those values. However, culture depends on interest, style and the particular values that are emphasised. There is more than one way to have a healthy culture, but I don't believe there is any room for exclusivity.

Ways to avoid this: set yourself a diversity target for recruiting and promoting, and encourage a culture of openness and transparency.

Summary

There are five main traps that I have witnessed or made. They are:

- ☐ We hold a big launch... and it's received with weariness and cynicism. A gradual embedding of values will be better received, unless the launch is at a time where there is significant evidence of behavioural change amongst the management team.

- ☐ Leaders don't live the values. This will result in a 'do as I say not as I do' situation. Leaders must examine their own behaviour in light of the values first.

- ☐ We don't involve non-management staff. Engaging with our staff is key to this process working as they are more likely to choose to behave in a way that reflects our values.

- ☐ We expect quick financial results. Whilst creating a positive culture is likely to bring success, linking this process to short-term financial targets is unlikely to work.

- ☐ Our culture becomes exclusive. When you have created your own unique culture that is working positively, there is a danger that you wrongly exclude others. It's important to remain transparent and open to feedback.

Action Checklist 6

Which of the above traps do you think you are most liable to fall into?

....
....
....

How are you going to avoid it?

....
....
....

Final Word

There is a growing awareness that staff who are happy and ful-filled, and who find meaning in their work, are more productive. Therefore, intentionally creating a culture in which people can thrive makes business sense. As leaders we play a crucial part in helping people to find meaning in their work by creating the right conditions – a workplace culture – for them to flourish.

APPENDIX A: Self-Assessment Questionnaires

To assess yourself against these seven leadership qualities give yourself a score between 1 (strongly disagree) and 10 (most agree) to the following statements.

How Resilient am I?

When I feel stressed:
I am aware of the people and situations that have triggered the stress

1 2 3 4 5 6 7 8 9 10

When I feel stressed:
I have strategies to manage it

1 2 3 4 5 6 7 8 9 10

When I feel stressed:
I am good at self-care, recharging my batteries

1 2 3 4 5 6 7 8 9 10

When I feel stressed:
I tell someone, and ask for help if necessary

1 2 3 4 5 6 7 8 9 10

During a period of sustained pressure:
I am able to keep going or if I crash I bounce back

1 2 3 4 5 6 7 8 9 10

If events lead to my workload increasing:
I can adapt and re-prioritise

1 2 3 4 5 6 7 8 9 10

In an emotionally charged situation:
I am able to stay engaged and manage my emotions

    1 2 3 4 5 6 7 8 9 10

When the unexpected crisis occurs:
I can face up to the situation and remain positive and hopeful

    1 2 3 4 5 6 7 8 9 10

How Empowering am I?

In terms of my team members' strengths:
It's my responsibility to find out what they are

    1 2 3 4 5 6 7 8 9 10

With the individuals in my team:
I regularly look for opportunities to enable them to use their strengths in their roles

    1 2 3 4 5 6 7 8 9 10

At review meetings/supervision:
I ask what, why, how questions and I speak no more than 30% of the time

    1 2 3 4 5 6 7 8 9 10

Most of the time, when it comes to delegation:
The outcomes are met or are above my expectations

    1 2 3 4 5 6 7 8 9 10

If one of the team messes something up:
We learn from it and try again

    1 2 3 4 5 6 7 8 9 10

In times of cost-cutting:
I fight to retain everyone, but prioritise those staff with potential

1 2 3 4 5 6 7 8 9 10

When asked what to do in a situation:
I ask for my team's suggestions first

1 2 3 4 5 6 7 8 9 10

I recruit and promote those:
Who have the potential to overtake me

1 2 3 4 5 6 7 8 9 10

How Emotionally Intelligent am I?

In terms of feedback:
I regularly invite feedback from my team

1 2 3 4 5 6 7 8 9 10

When my team or an individual challenges me:
I consider their feedback carefully and make changes to my behaviour and actions if necessary

1 2 3 4 5 6 7 8 9 10

If I'm in a bad mood:
I leave it at home, not letting it influence me at work

1 2 3 4 5 6 7 8 9 10

If someone is dominating a meeting:
I am able to manage the dynamics and involve the quieter members

1 2 3 4 5 6 7 8 9 10

If something is bothering me:
I will talk it over with a trusted colleague if necessary, and get on with my day

   1 2 3 4 5 6 7 8 9 10

In emotionally charged situations:
I remain engaged but don't get drawn in

   1 2 3 4 5 6 7 8 9 10

When someone is talking to me:
Where possible, I give them my full attention and make eye contact

   1 2 3 4 5 6 7 8 9 10

When I am anxious:
I can think of ways to calm myself down

   1 2 3 4 5 6 7 8 9 10

How good a Decision-Maker am I?

When making a decision:
I make it in good time

   1 2 3 4 5 6 7 8 9 10

When making a decision:
I'm prepared to occasionally get it wrong

   1 2 3 4 5 6 7 8 9 10

When making decisions:
I'm aware of my decision-making style

   1 2 3 4 5 6 7 8 9 10

When I've made a decision:
I stick to it except in exceptional circumstances

1 2 3 4 5 6 7 8 9 10

When making crucial decisions:
I seek the opinion of one or two key people

1 2 3 4 5 6 7 8 9 10

When making decisions that may make me unpopular with my team:
I'm not afraid to do so

1 2 3 4 5 6 7 8 9 10

When making such decisions (as above):
I carefully consider how I'm going to communicate the decision

1 2 3 4 5 6 7 8 9 10

How good a Communicator am I?

When I ask my team for some information or a piece of work:
I generally get what I've asked for

1 2 3 4 5 6 7 8 9 10

When I ask my team to give me feedback:
They give it to me

1 2 3 4 5 6 7 8 9 10

When faced with difficult conversations or conflict:
I don't shy away from them

1 2 3 4 5 6 7 8 9 10

When approaching a disagreement or emotionally charged situation:
I seek first to listen and understand

   1 2 3 4 5 6 7 8 9 10

When I get an emotionally charged email:
I phone them at the earliest opportunity

   1 2 3 4 5 6 7 8 9 10

If there is a performance issue in my team I:
Arrange to meet with them ASAP

   1 2 3 4 5 6 7 8 9 10

My emails are:
Respectful, but to the point

   1 2 3 4 5 6 7 8 9 10

How Visionary am I?

In terms of the future:
I can visualise my role/team/organisation being bigger better, stronger or different

   1 2 3 4 5 6 7 8 9 10

In terms of the vision:
I know how to take it and turn it into a strategy for change

   1 2 3 4 5 6 7 8 9 10

When unexpected change occurs:
I remain positive and hopeful, keeping my eyes on the bigger picture

1 2 3 4 5 6 7 8 9 10

When problems arise:
I see them as opportunities for creative solutions

1 2 3 4 5 6 7 8 9 10

In terms of communicating the strategy:
I am able to communicate it, in timescales outcomes, people, budgets etc.

1 2 3 4 5 6 7 8 9 10

If circumstances change:
I can adapt the strategy in response

1 2 3 4 5 6 7 8 9 10

How Courageous am I?

When setting goals for my team:
They are ambitious, as with the right support I believe the team can rise to the challenge

1 2 3 4 5 6 7 8 9 10

When it comes to taking action on a new idea:
I more often take the first step towards it

1 2 3 4 5 6 7 8 9 10

Regarding my performance and behaviour:
I am transparent about my mistakes and weaknesses

1 2 3 4 5 6 7 8 9 10

Regarding the choosing of my team:
I deliberately employ people who are different to me, who challenge and question me

1 2 3 4 5 6 7 8 9 10

When challenges arise:
I persist until I find a way to solve them

1 2 3 4 5 6 7 8 9 10

EVALUATION:

If you have circled answers 6–10 on any questions, it is an indication that you have some further development to do in those areas.

About the author

Vanessa O'Shea is the founder of Culture Shapers, a consultancy designed to help companies shape a healthy and positive culture. After working in the field of HR for over 20 years, and observing the impact on staff, of changes in direction, leadership and growth, she left her job to concentrate on researching, designing and trialling a model for shaping culture. This is the book she would have wanted to have read five years ago.

Vanessa consults in both charities and the for-profit sector and delivers workshops on culture shaping and leadership development.

Vanessa loves to run and play her cello (but not at the same time). She lives in Brighton, UK with her husband; she has two grown-up children.

Notes

Chapter 1
Workplace Culture: What it Means and Why it Matters

1 Brene Brown, *Daring Greatly*, Penguin Life, 2012.

2 Bob Chapman and Raj Sisodia, *Everybody Matters*, Penguin Random House, 2015.

3 Tom Rath, *Strengthsfinder*, Gallup Press, 2007.

4 Mark Twain quote taken from *Strengthsfinder*, by Tom Rath, Gallup Press.

Chapter 3
What: Mission

5 www.pursuitmarketing.co.uk

6 This model of culture-shaping was designed by the author and delivered in full whilst she was working for a Sussex charity. For more information and case studies, see her website : https://www.cultureshapers.co.uk

7 Simon Sinek, *Start with Why: How Great Leaders Inspire Everyone to Take Action*, Penguin, 2011.

8 Costa Coffee is a British multi-national coffee house company. https://www.costa.co.uk

9 John Lewis group is a chain of department stores operating in the UK. https://www.johnlewis.com/

10 Walt Disney is an international entertainment and media enterprise and is the world's largest media company. https://www.thewaltdisneycompany.com/

11 Martin Luther King was an American Baptist minister and activist who became the most visible spokesperson

and leader in the civil rights movement from 1954 until his death in 1968.

12 William Wilberforce was a deeply religious English politician and social reformer, who led the abolition of the slave trade, and eventually slavery itself in the British Empire.

13 Millicent Fawcett was a leading suffragist and campaigner for equal rights for women. She led the biggest suffrage organisation, and played a key role in gaining women the vote.

14 John Spedan Lewis turned the famous department store chain founded by his father John Lewis into a partnership with his staff, as an experiment to create a better way of managing business.

15 JK Rowling, is a British novelist, most famous for writing the Harry Potter fantasy series. The first book was allegedly written from a café in Edinburgh, Scotland.

Chapter 4
Why: Values

16 Jim Collins, *Good to Great*, Random House Business Books, 2001

17 Brightec is a business that develops mobile apps based in Brighton, Sussex, England. www.brightec.co.uk

18 Hewlett Packard (HP) is an American multi-national computer and electronics company, based in California, USA. www.hp.com

19 Brighton Table Tennis Club is a charity that uses table tennis to bring communities together and transform lives. www.brightontabletennisclub.co.uk

20 Spotify is a digital streaming service, with headquarters in Sweden. www.spotify.com

21 Brene Brown, *Daring Greatly*, Penguin Life, 2012.

Chapter 5
How (Part 1): Embedding our Values

22 The Joseph Rowntree Foundation, is an independent social change organisation working to solve poverty in the UK. www.jrf.org.uk

23 E&W YMCA is a charity that provides holistic support to young, vulnerable people. www.ewymca.org

Chapter 6
How: (Part 2): Six Ways to Embed our Values

24 Jim Collins, Good to Great, Random House Business Books, 2001.

25 Stav Ziv, 10 Traits of a Great Manager according to Google's Internal Research, The Muse, www.themuse.com

26 Brightec See www.brightec.com.

Chapter 7
Who: Equipping Managers: Seven Qualities of a Culture-Shaping Leader

27 Extroversion and Introversion.

Myers Briggs group have developed this idea comprehensively. Their practitioners (I am one) can access questionnaires, create reports and provide coaching on how you can use the information in the reports to develop your working style.

www.cultureshapers.co.uk (my website)

https://eu.themyersbriggs.com/en (Myers Briggs Group website)

28 A groundbreaking book written from the perspective of an introvert is:

Susan Cain, *Quiet: The Power of Introverts in a World That Can't Stop Talking*, Penguin, 2013.

15356700R00076

Printed in Great Britain
by Amazon